STICK CONTROL

for the

SNARE DRUMMER

The Colonial Drummer

By *GEORGE LAWRENCE STONE*

Nationally Known Authority on Rudimental Drumming
Principal of the Stone Drum and Xylophone School of Boston
and Drum Editor of "The International Musician" 1946–1963

Exclusively Distributed by

Alfred

alfred.com

©2009 STONE PERCUSSION BOOKS® LLC

◄[STONE PERCUSSION BOOKS® LLC]►

ORIGINALLY PUBLISHED BY GEORGE B. STONE & SON, INC.

www.stonepercussionbooks.com
stonepercussionbooks@comcast.net

3/2022

GEORGE LAWRENCE STONE
1886–1967

GEORGE LAWRENCE STONE was born on November 1st, 1886, in South Boston, the only child of George Burt Stone (1856–1917, left) and Abigail Stone. The elder Stone was a well-known performer and instructor who opened George B. Stone & Son, Inc. in 1890 for the manufacture of drums, traps, and accessories. George Lawrence soon followed in his father's footsteps, working in the Stone "office and manufactory" on Hanover Street in Boston, eventually taking over the family business and expanding into the publication of percussion instruction books (see back cover for a list of titles).

George Lawrence Stone joined the musician's union at the age of 16 as its youngest member. He played solo xylophone on the Keith Vaudeville Circuit, served in the 1st Corps Cadets, Massachusetts Volunteer Militia as a regimental drummer, played with the Boston Grand Opera Company, the Boston Festival Orchestra, and at Boston's Colonial Theater, and worked with a number of other performing groups. In 1933 he was one of the founding members of NARD (National Association of Rudimentary Drummers), ran the Stone Drum and Xylophone School in Boston, and wrote five books on percussion, including *Stick Control for the Snare Drummer.* He judged competitions, wrote articles, lectured, taught and played throughout his professional life. In 1940 the Jacobs Orchestra Monthly reported "It is to be presumed that he sleeps and eats, but when or how this is managed has never been divulged, at least not to us."

Many a drummer knows Stone's *Stick Control for the Snare Drummer* as an essential part of their learning library, and as their "bible of drumming." The followup book to *Stick Control, Accents & Rebounds for the Snare Drummer,* was inspired by then-student and now legendary musician Joe Morello's addition of accents to the lessons in *Stick Control.*

Even later in life George Lawrence Stone kept working hours to continue to practice and write. In 1967 Stone died at the age of 81, two days before the death of his wife Paulina. In 1997 Stone was inducted into the PAS (Percussion Arts Society) Hall of Fame. Some descendants still remember taking childhood lessons using *Stick Control*, testing the accuracy of their rolls with the carbon paper test under the watchful eye of their grandfather—joining countless students, teachers, and professionals around the world who continue to be inspired by the guidance and lessons of George Lawrence Stone.

Above left: George Lawrence Stone as a Keith xylophonist; *center,* in a brochure used to promote Stone's percussion lectures; *right,* as he appeared in the 1940s in materials used by NARD, the National Association of Rudimentary Drummers, which selected and standardized the Thirteen Essential Rudiments. Stone was a founding NARD member and president of the organization from 1945 to 1954.

Photos courtesy Stone Percussion Books® LLC

PREFACE

It seems that there are too many drummers whose work is of a rough-and-ready variety and whose technical proficiency suffers in comparison with that of the players of other instruments.

Of course, technical proficiency can come only through continued, well-directed practise. The more practise one does the more proficiency he acquires.

Many concert pianists practise hours and hours every day. They continue practising after they graduate from the student period and enter into the professional field. Violinists, cornetists and the players of other instruments do likewise. Through regular and systematic practise they "keep in shape."

To the uninitiated, the art of drumming appears easy—so easy in fact that unless the drum student has had the advantage of expert advice, he may fail to realize the importance of the long hours of hard, painstaking practise that must be put in before he is technically prepared to enter the professional field with the confidence that his efforts will measure up to approved musical standards.

However, in defence of the drummer, let it be noted that while the pianist and violinist have access to many hundreds of elementary and advanced text-books, covering every known branch of their art, the drummer's library is limited to a score or so of instruction books, and not all of these containing the specific type, or generous amount of practise material necessary to the development of that high degree of fundamental mechanical dexterity required from the modern drummer.

It is in realization of this need and in answer to requests from drum instructors in all parts of the country that this series of practise-rhythms has been prepared and presented herewith under the title of:—

"STICK CONTROL—For The Snare Drummer"

"STICK CONTROL" is a highly specialized practise-book, dealing with just one branch of the art of drumming. It is an advanced book, consisting of a progressive, highly concentrated collection of rhythms, arranged in calisthenic form, which, if practised regularly and intelligently, will enable one to acquire control, speed, flexibility, touch, rhythm, lightness, delicacy, power, endurance, preciseness of execution and muscular co-ordination to a degree far in excess of his present ability.

"STICK CONTROL" is intended to develop finger, wrist, and arm muscles, which to the rudimental drummer, playing in exhibition or contest, means speed, power and endurance, and to the orchestral drummer, specializing in lighter types of playing, means clean, crisp execution, precise interpretation and flexibility of control, especially in the "pianissimo" rolls and delicate shading.

"STICK CONTROL" contains a wealth of material for the development of the drummer's weak or awkward hand (which to the right handed individual is his left), thereby enabling him to acquire ambidexterity in a sufficient degree for smooth, rhythmic hand-to-hand execution. Its stick-work being entirely mechanical in scope, "STICK CONTROL" does not conflict with any of the known "systems" of drumming, therefore any instructor may assign its pages, at his discretion, concurrently with his regular assignment to the pupil. The expert instructor will find in the rhythms of "STICK CONTROL" an abundance of material designed to make his own daily "work-out" more interesting and productive.

An hour a day with "STICK CONTROL" will work wonders for one, whether he be rudimental exhibitionist or concert drummer; student or expert; jazz drummer or symphonist. The only vital requirement for this book (or, indeed, for any drum instruction book) is regular practise; and, to the student, the author recommends the services of a local expert instructor, whenever such services are available.

GEORGE LAWRENCE STONE

Original preface to the 1935 edition of *Stick Control for the Snare Drummer* by George Lawrence Stone

HOW TO PRACTISE "STICK CONTROL"

It will be noted that the practise-rhythms in "STICK CONTROL" are numbered and are without the customary musical ending. This is so that each rhythm may be practised over and over before proceeding to the next one, which method of practise is the most conducive to quick and satisfactory results.

The author recommends that each rhythm be practised 20 TIMES WITHOUT STOPPING. Then go on to the next one. THIS IS IMPORTANT. "STICK CONTROL" cannot serve its purpose as well in any other way.

Practise with the metronome is also recommended, and at several different speeds, varying from extremely slow to extremely fast; and again without the metronome, in the open and closed style, i.e., starting very slowly, gradually accelerating to top speed, then slowing down again, finally ending at the original tempo.

Practise at all times with relaxed muscles, stopping at the slightest feeling of tension. Remember, the rhythms in "STICK CONTROL" are "conditioners." They are designed to give control. Control begins in muscularly relaxed action.

A WORD TO THE ORCHESTRAL DRUMMER:—Do not let the word "rudimental" frighten you nor prevent you from putting in a normal amount of practise on power, high-hand practise and the open roll. This will not spoil the light touch, delicate shading or fine-grained effects demanded of you in modern musical interpretation. To the contrary, by giving you a better control of the sticks, it will enable you to produce even finer and more delicate effects than heretofore.

LIKEWISE, A WORD TO THE RUDIMENTAL DRUMMER:—Do not hesitate to devote a portion of your practise period to lightness and touch, and especially to the playing of the closed roll, for if your practise is confined entirely to power and endurance your execution will become "one-sided," heavy and clumsy. Strange to say, practise in lighter execution will, by giving you a fuller control of the sticks, help your power, endurance, and speed.

The "open roll," referred to throughout the book (and beginning on page 11), is the rudimental roll of two beats (no more) of each stick, in rhythmic alternation.

The "closed roll," notated on page 12 and thereafter, is the one commonly used in light orchestral playing. It has several rebounds to each stick movement, instead of just one, this being produced by a slight additional pressure, applied to the sticks as the roll is executed. This closed roll is not to be confused with that exaggerated type of roll known as the "scratch roll," produced by digging the sticks down into the drumhead with muscles tense, at a ridiculously high rate of speed, for which neither the author, nor indeed any musician, has any use.

Practise each rhythm 20 TIMES WITHOUT STOPPING. Then go on to the next one.

Original introduction to the 1935 edition of *Stick Control for the Snare Drummer* by George Lawrence Stone

Stone Percussion Books® LLC, a family company owned by George Lawrence Stone's descendants,
would like to thank Dom Famularo for his help and encouragement in the reissue of this and other classic Stone percussion books.
For more information about Dom and his remarkable work in drumming, teaching, publishing,
and motivational workshops and events around the world, visit Dom's website at
www.domfamularo.com

Project Coordinators: Dom Famularo & Joe Bergamini
Layout and engraving: Willie Rose
Text layout: Barbara Haines, Stone Percussion Books® LLC
Editorial Consultant: Dave Black
Additional engraving: Stephane Chamberland

Single Beat Combinations

Repeat each exercise 20 times.

Single Beat Combinations

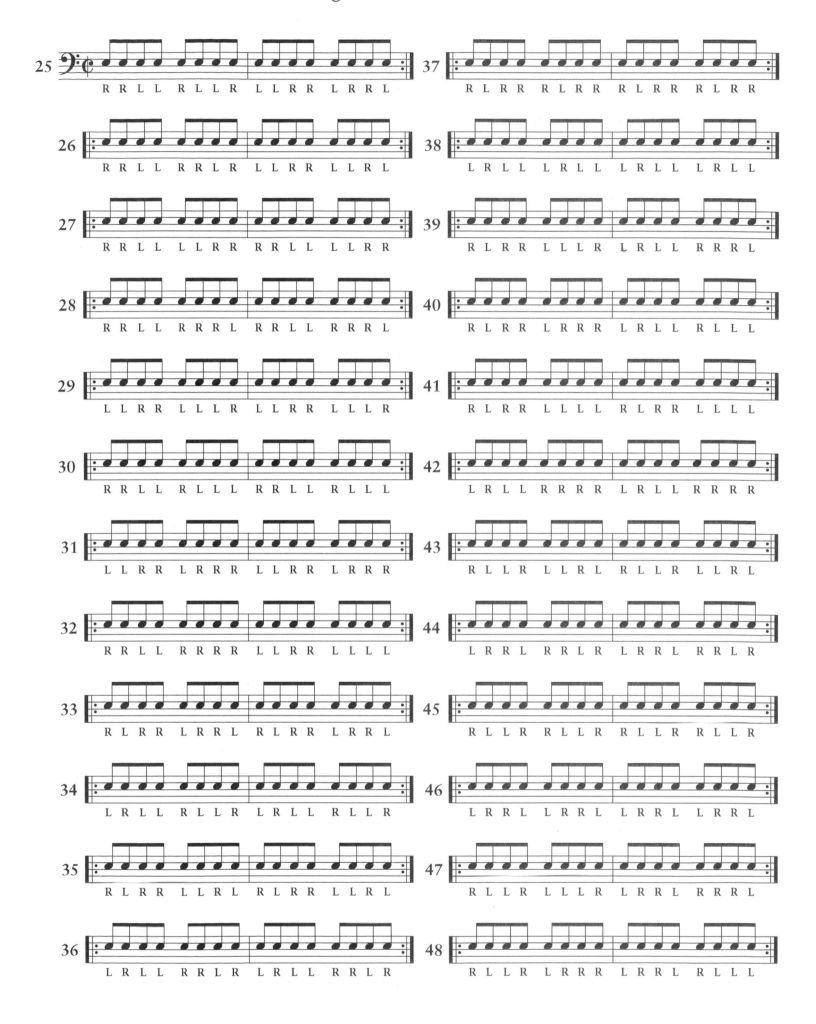

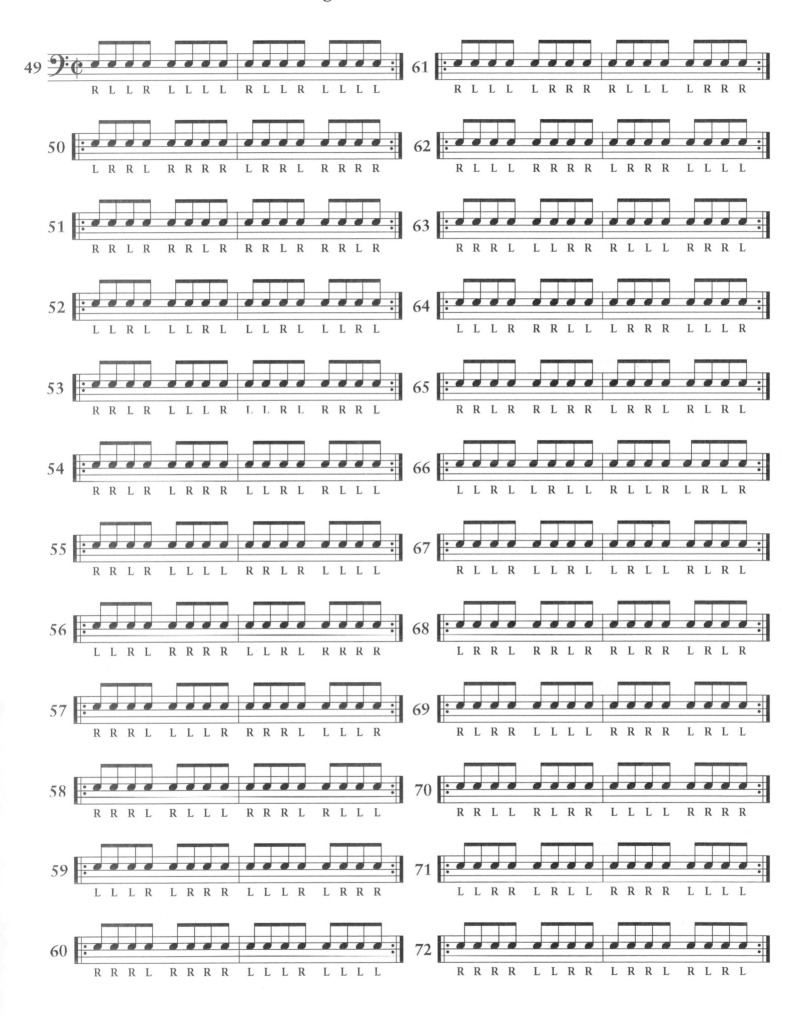

Triplets

Read downward

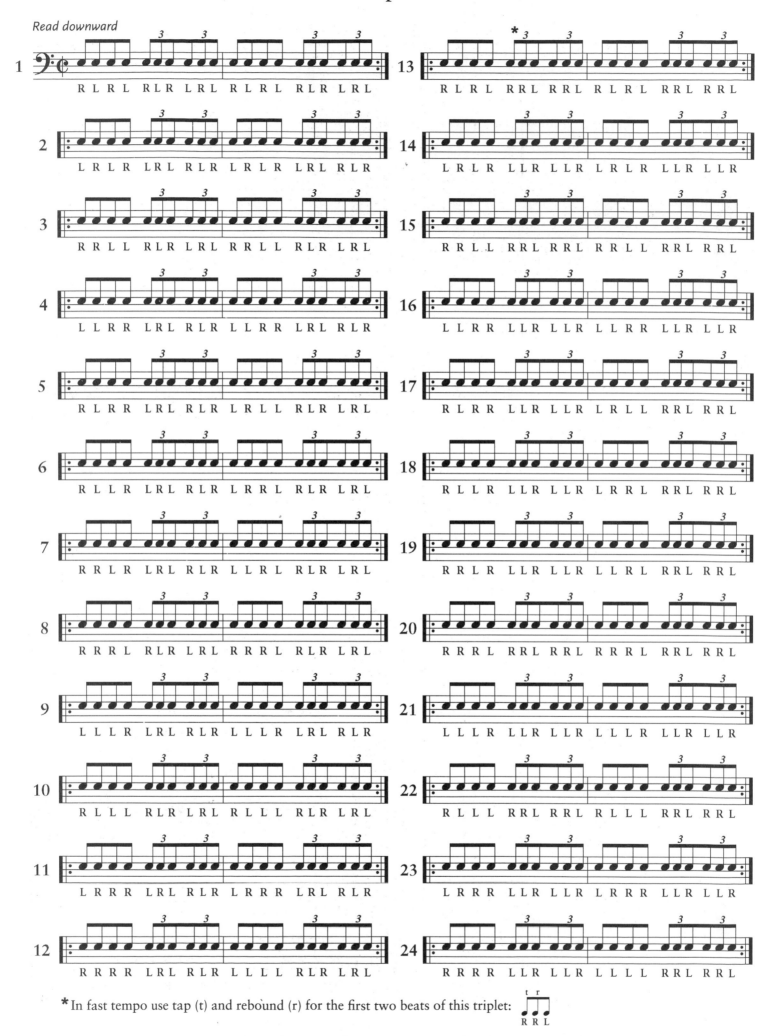

* In fast tempo use tap (t) and rebound (r) for the first two beats of this triplet:

Triplets

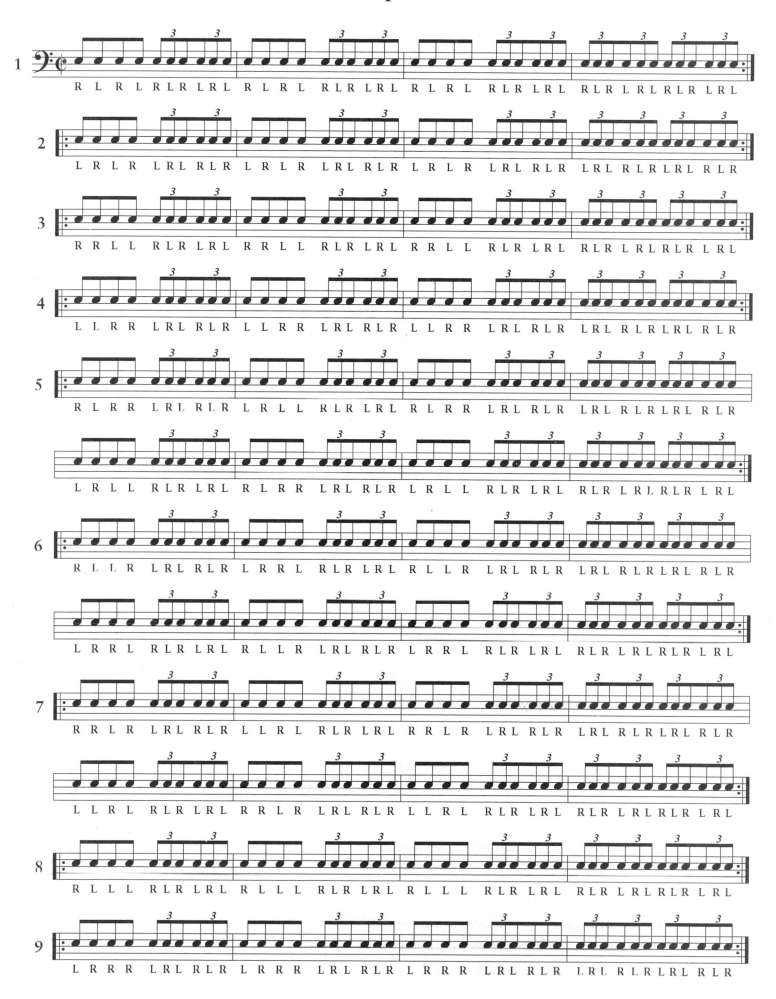

Short Roll Combinations (Single Beat Rolls)

Read downward

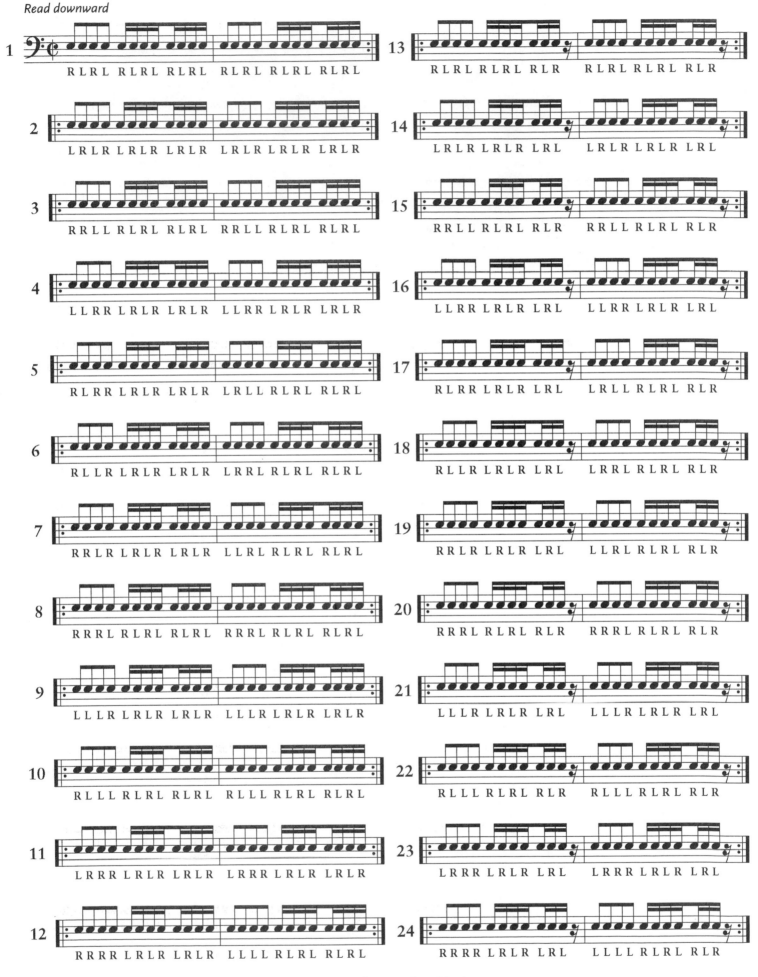

Repeat each exercise 20 times.

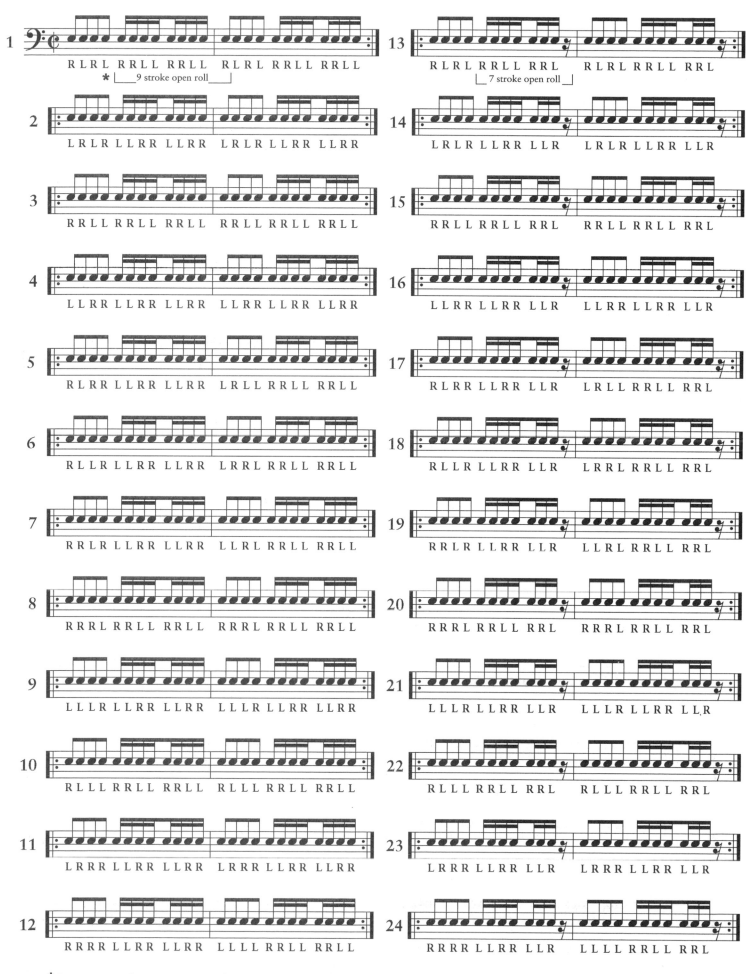

* See paragraph on page 4 explaining the "open roll"

Short Roll Combinations

*See paragraph on page 4 explaining the "closed roll"

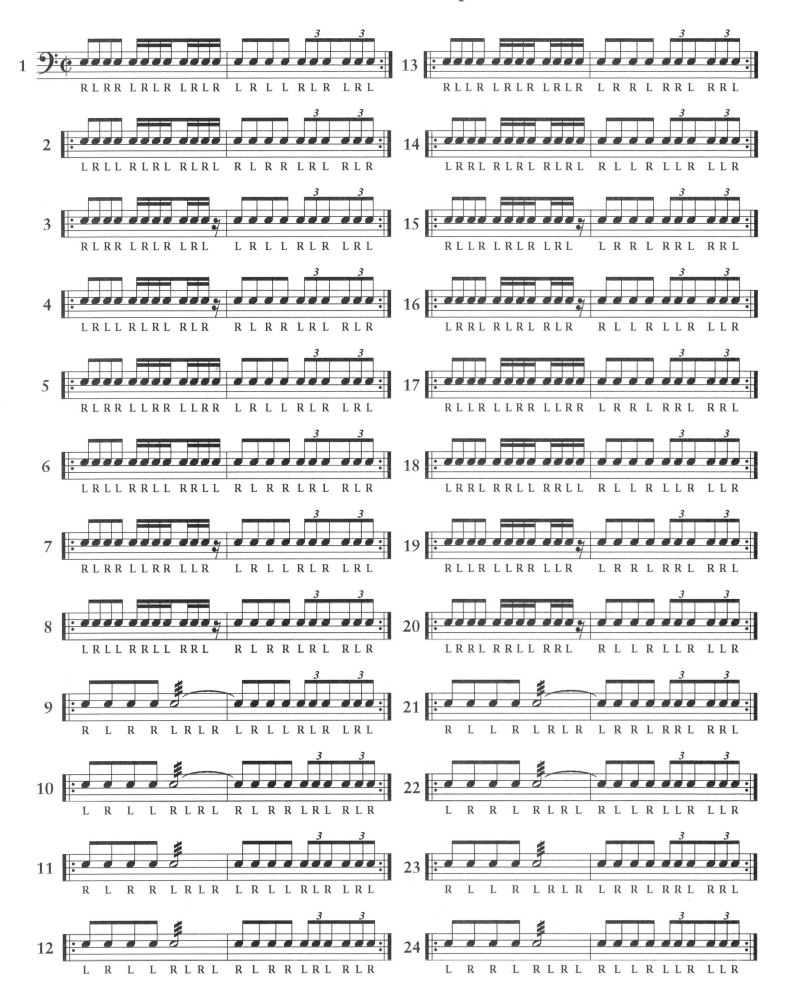

Flam Beats

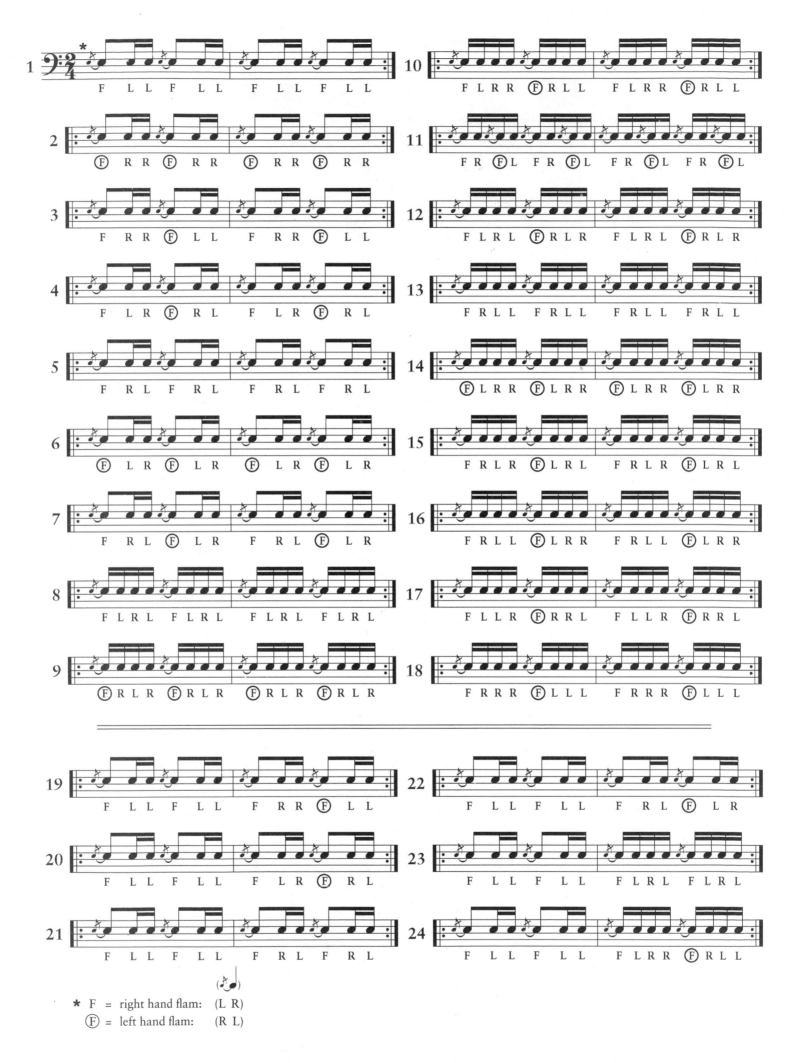

* F = right hand flam: (L R)
Ⓕ = left hand flam: (R L)

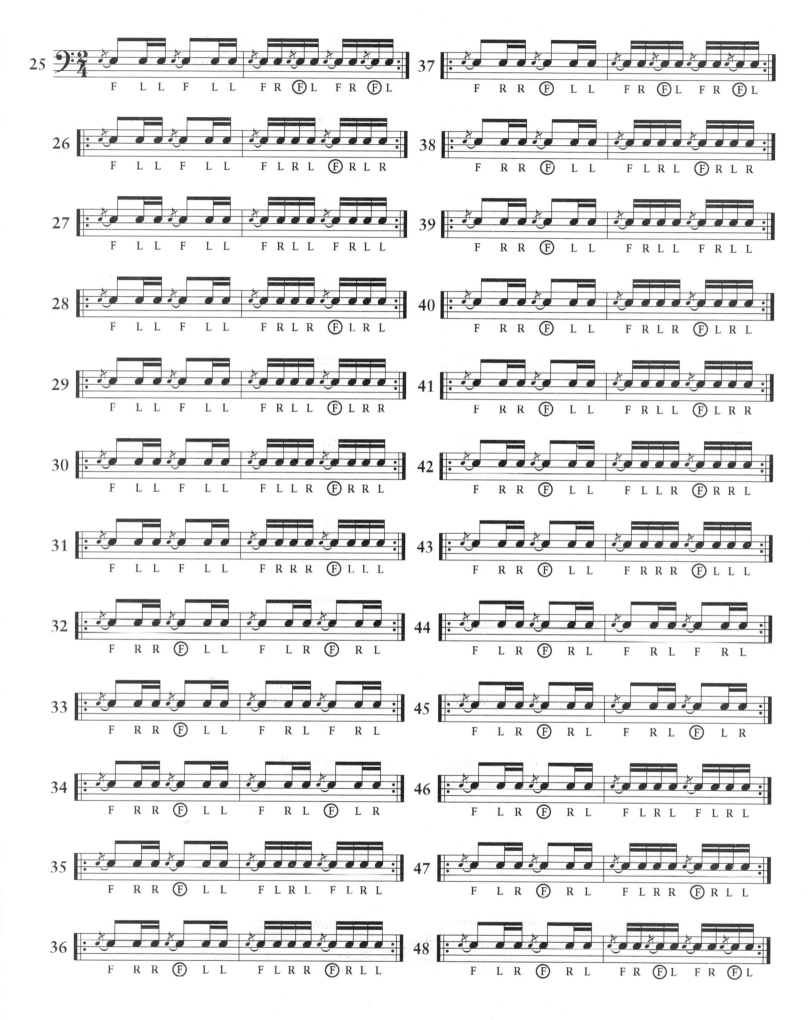

Flam Beats

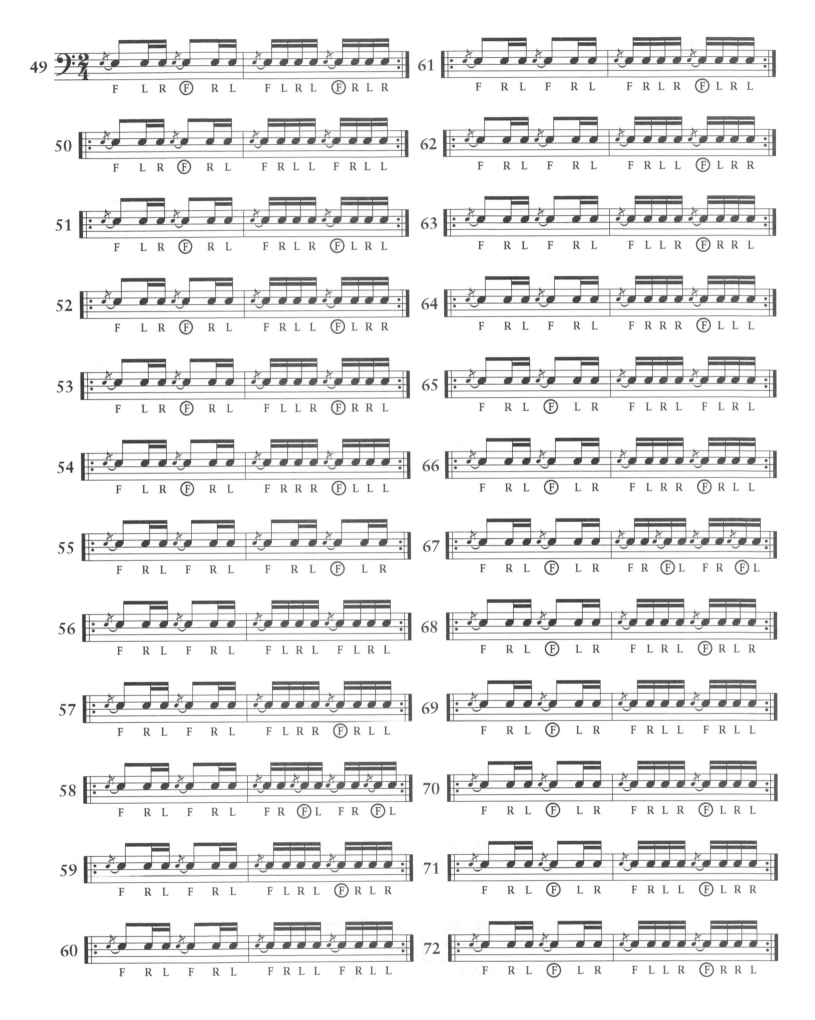

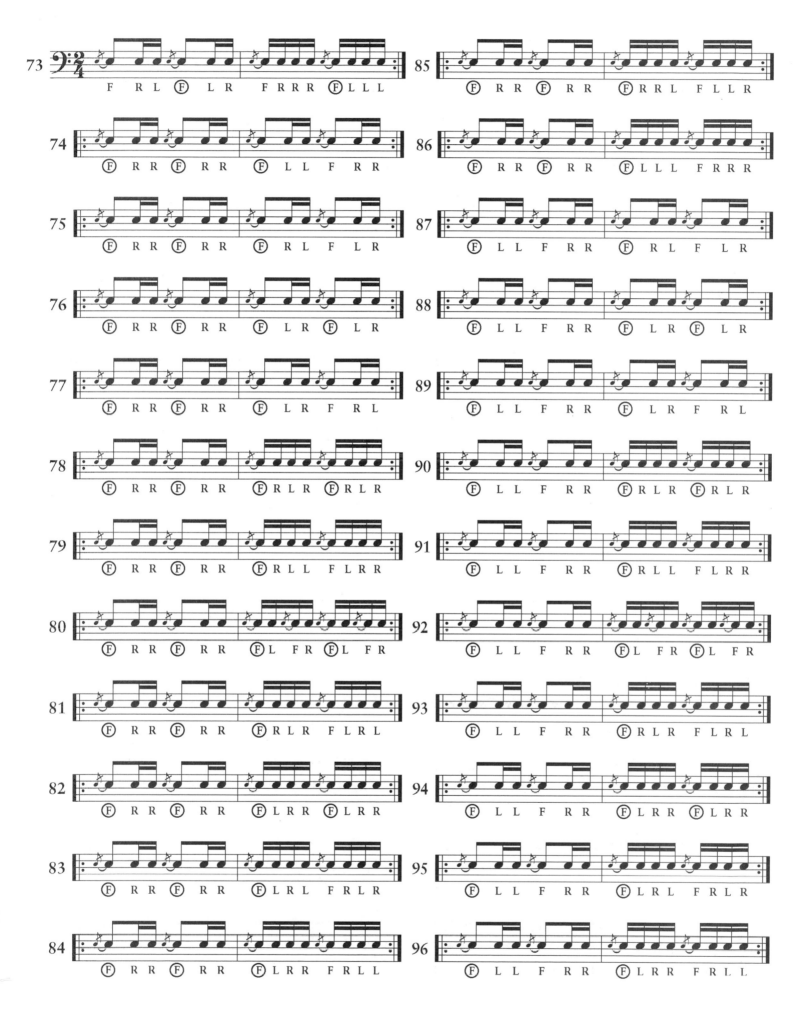

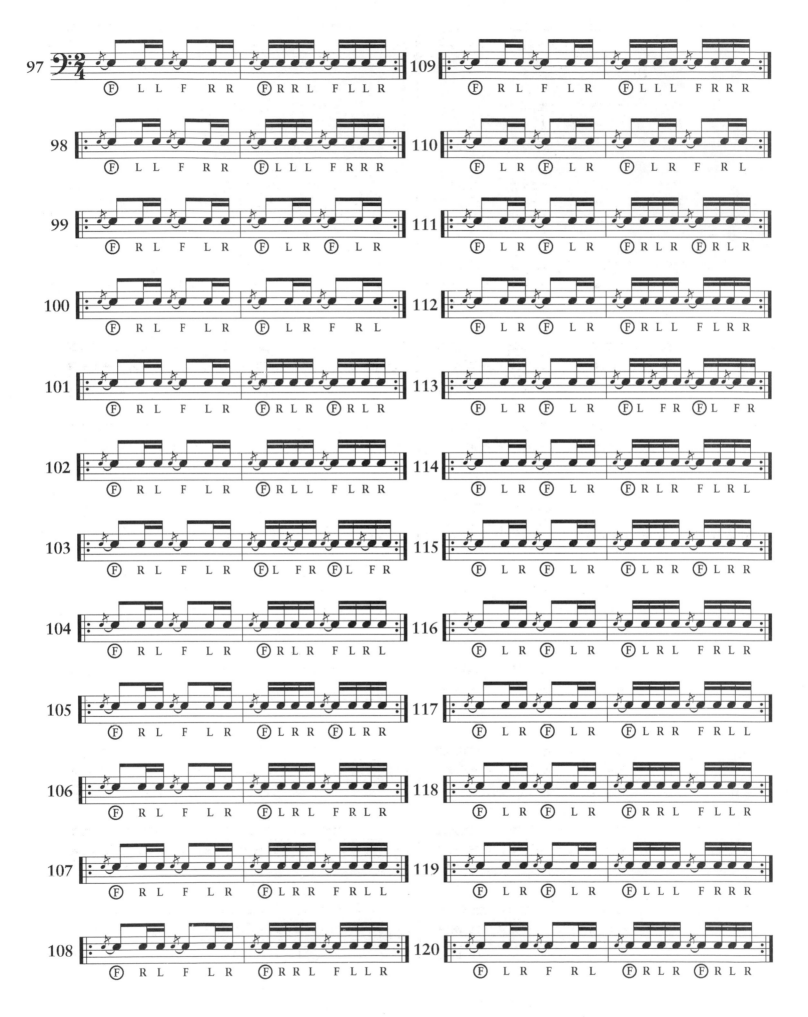

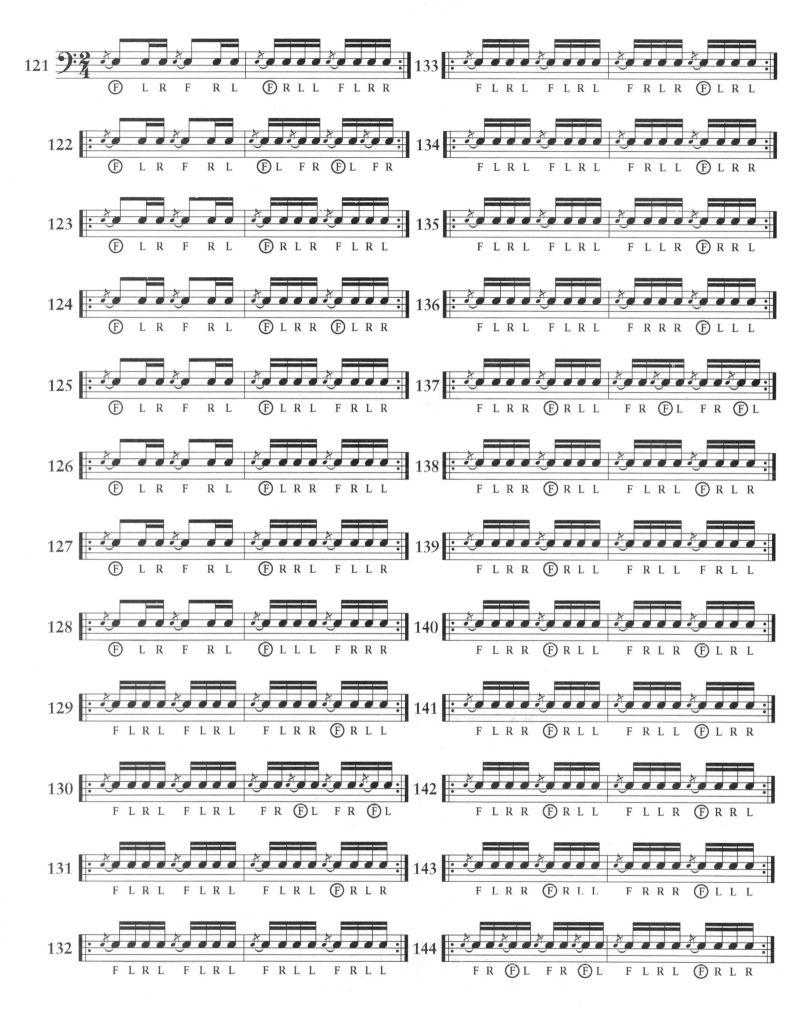

Flam Beats

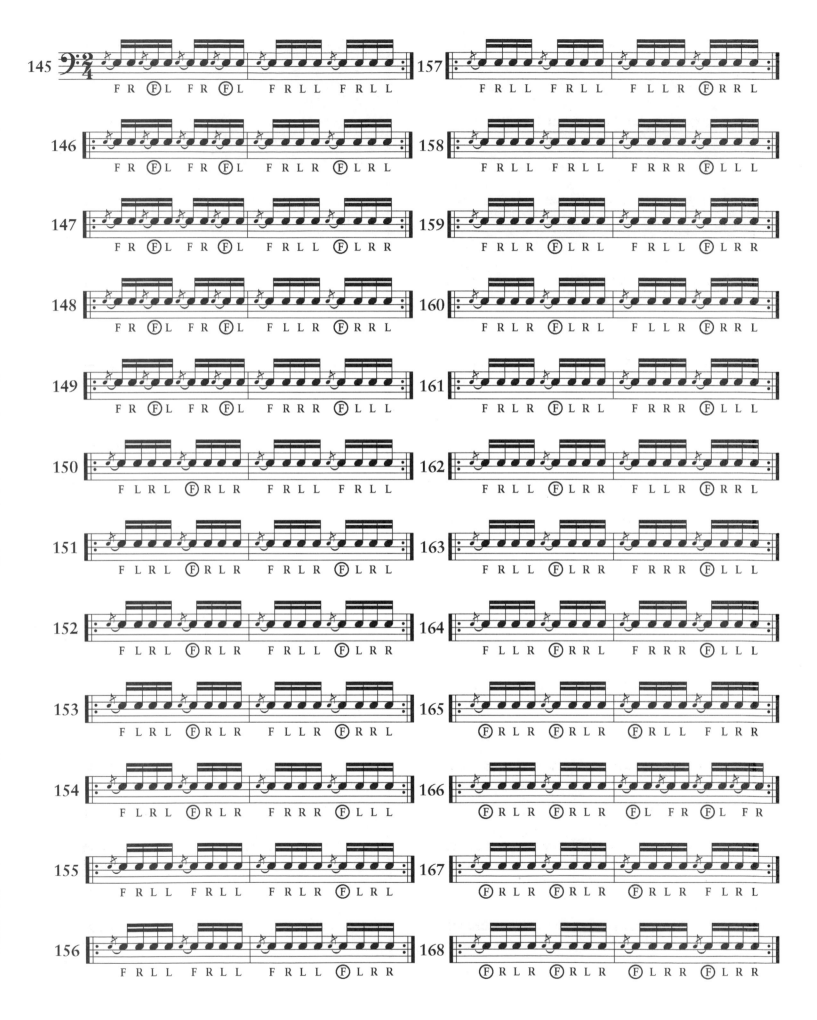

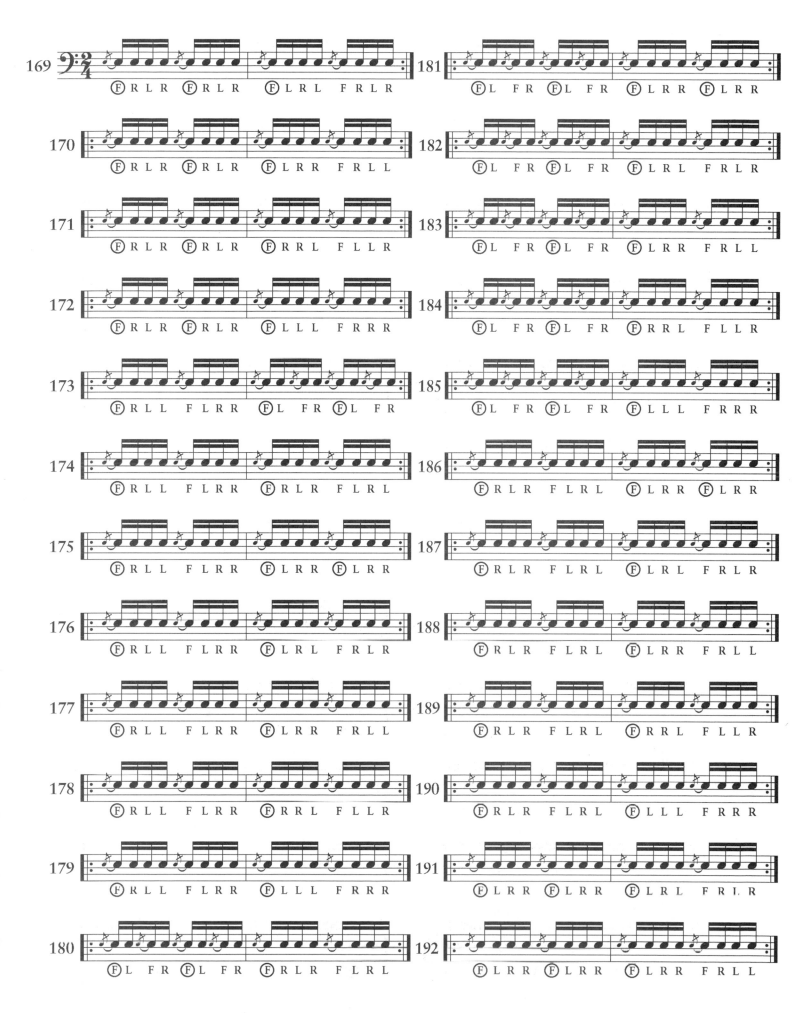

Short Rolls in 6/8

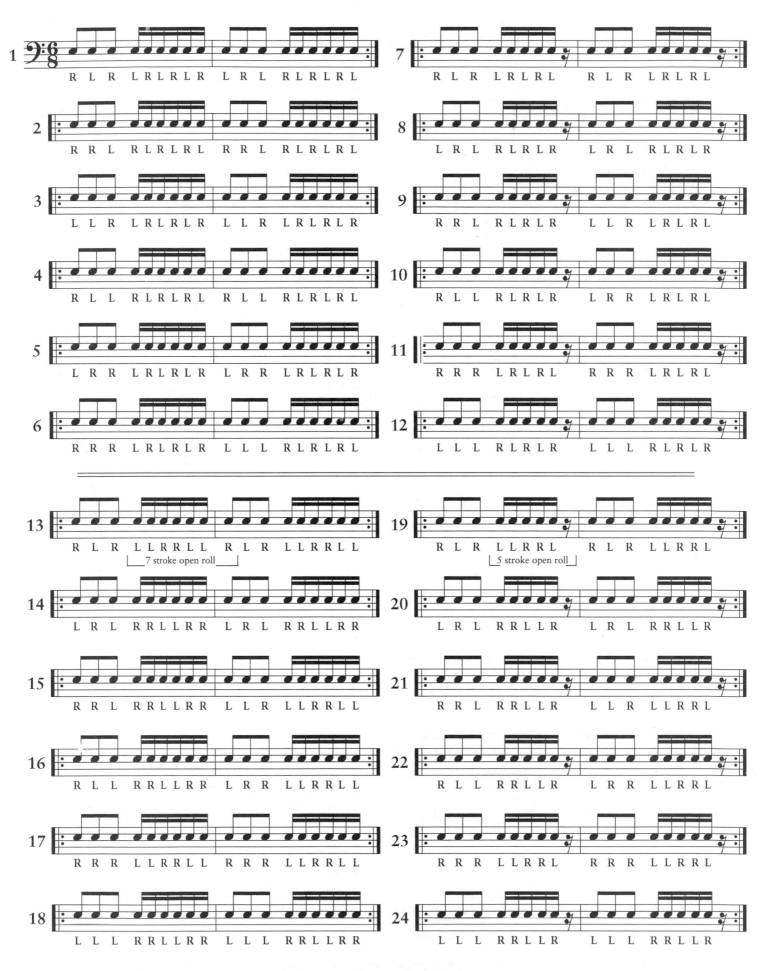

Repeat each exercise 20 times.

Short Rolls in 6/8

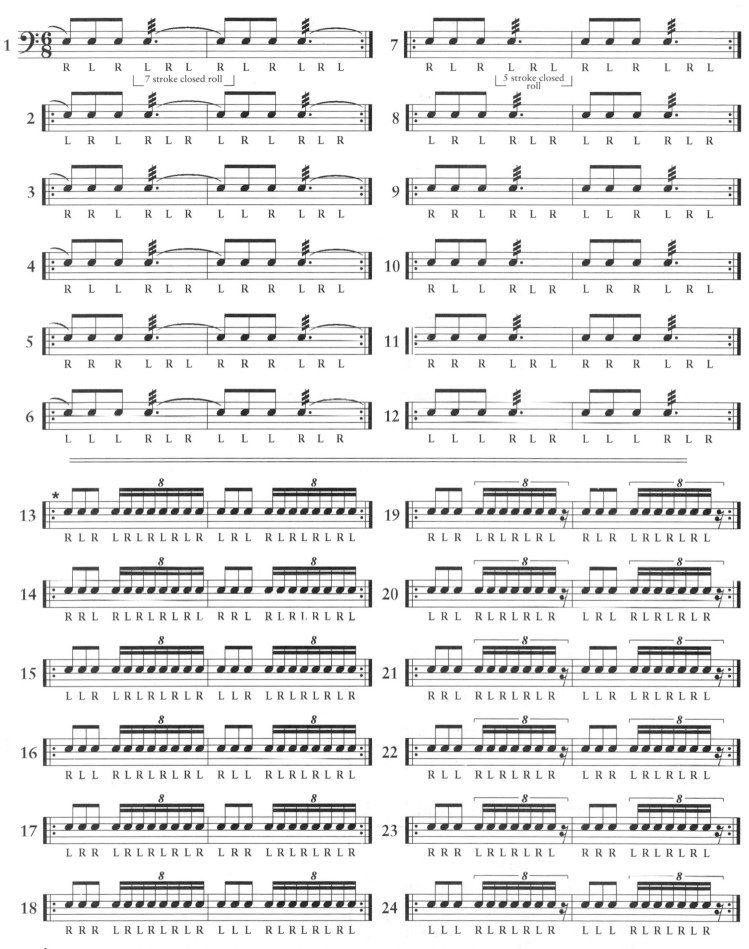

*The notation of this and of similar measures on pages 25 and 26, although irregular, seems to lead up in a more readable manner into the closed rolls on page 26. The precise notation of this measure should be as follows:

Short Rolls in 6/8

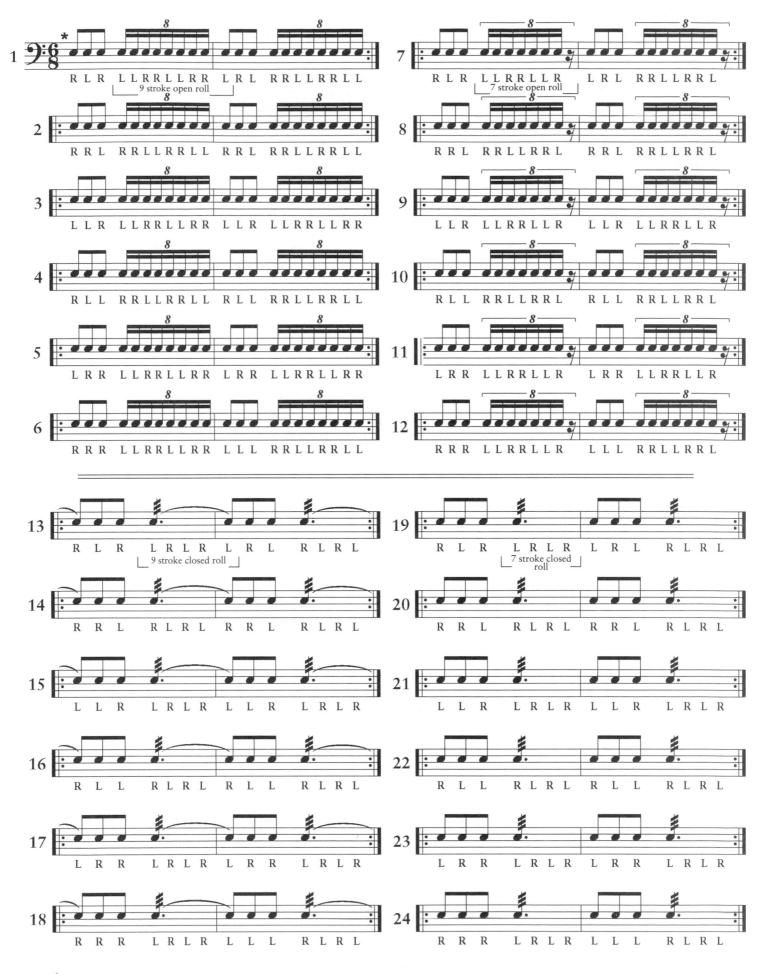

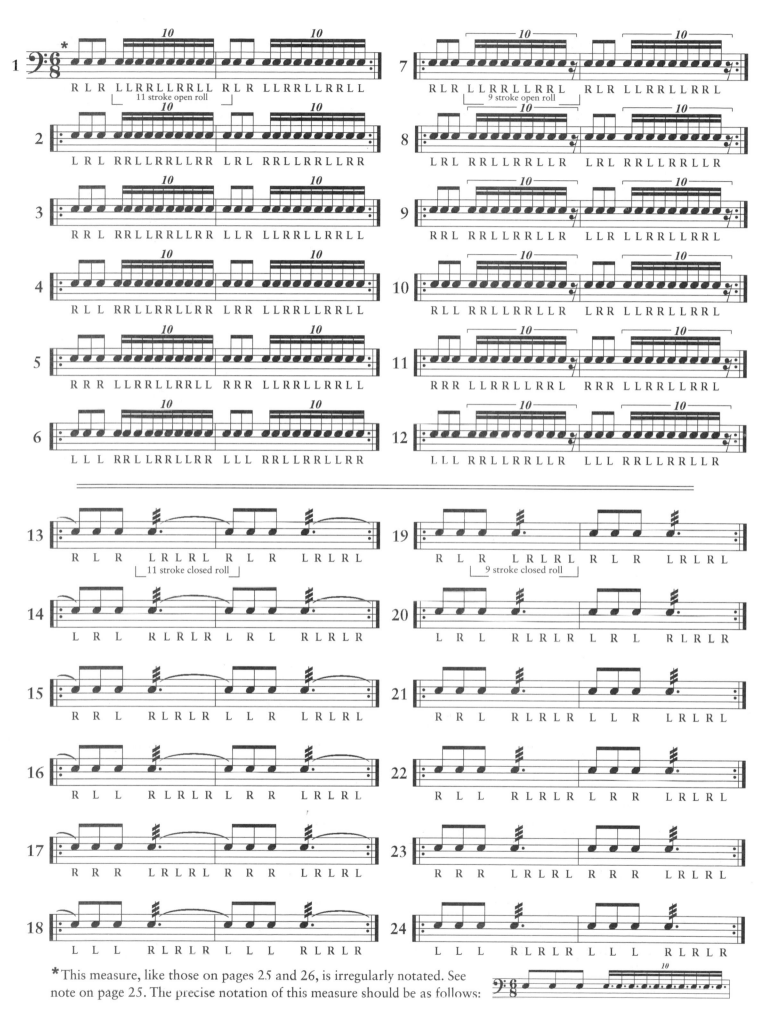

*This measure, like those on pages 25 and 26, is irregularly notated. See note on page 25. The precise notation of this measure should be as follows:

Review of Short Rolls in 6/8

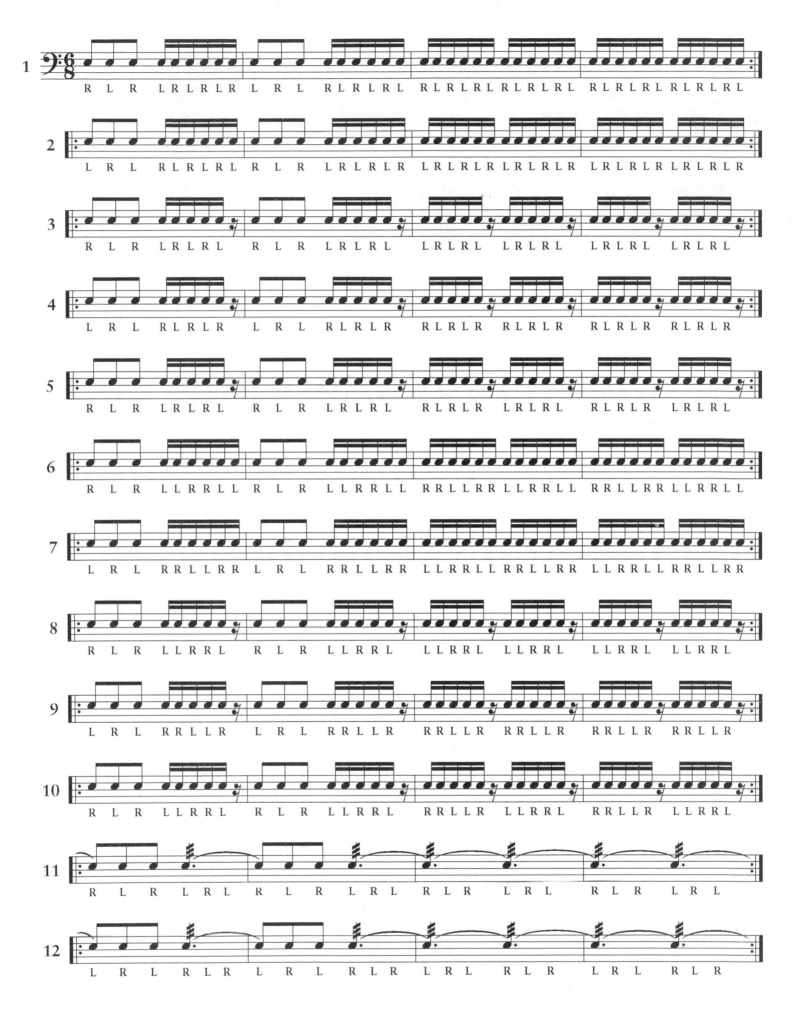

Review of Short Rolls in 6/8

Combinations in 3/8

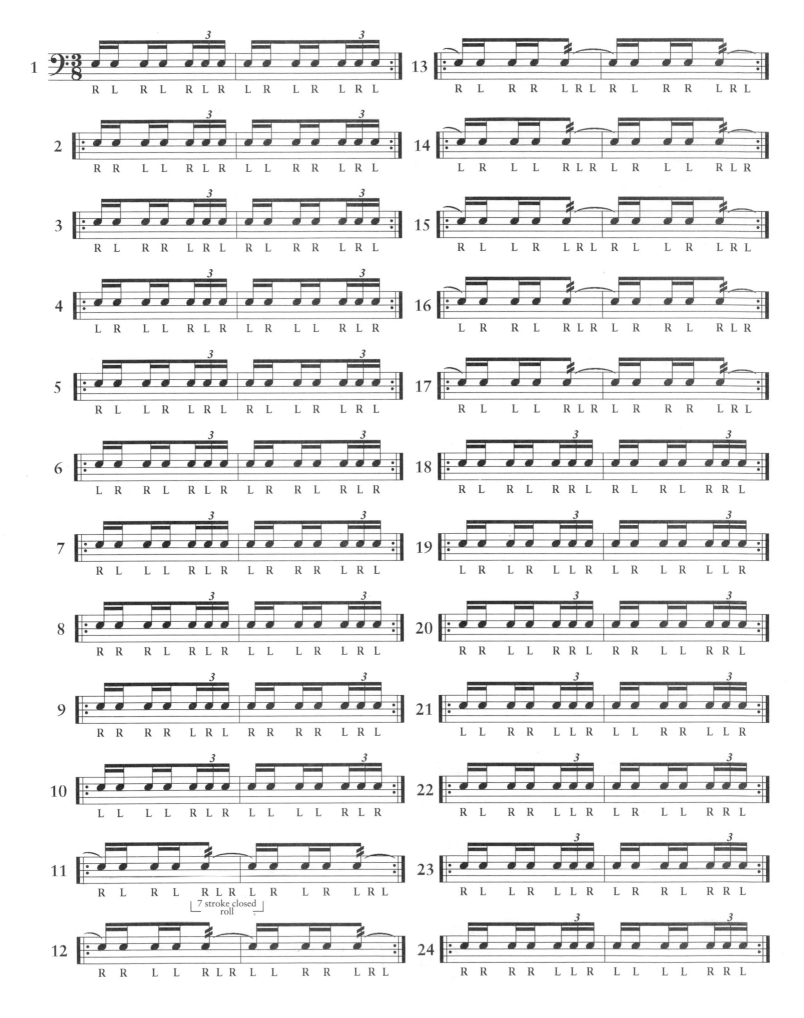

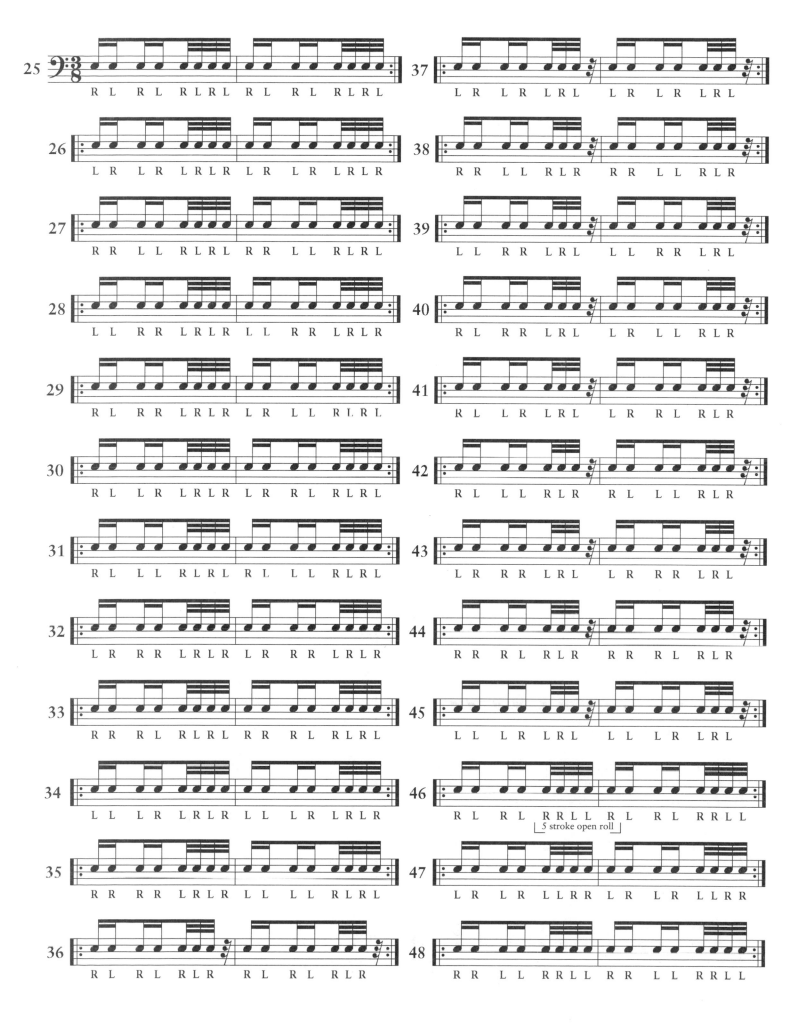

Combinations in 3/8

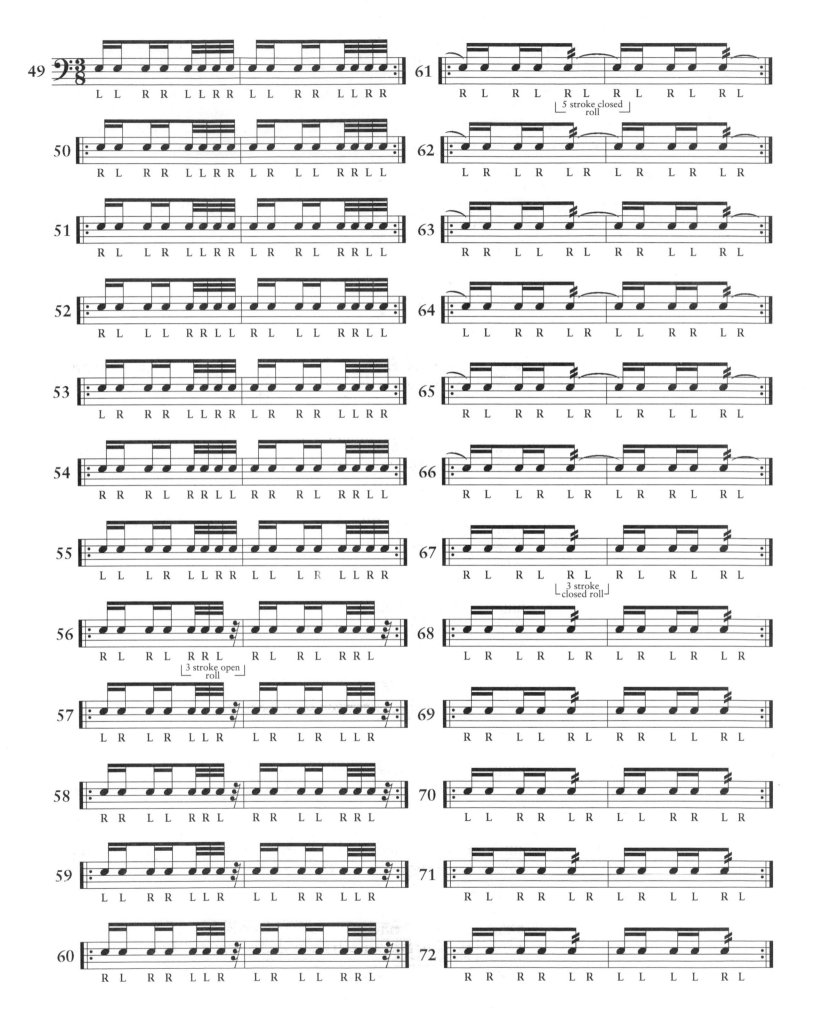

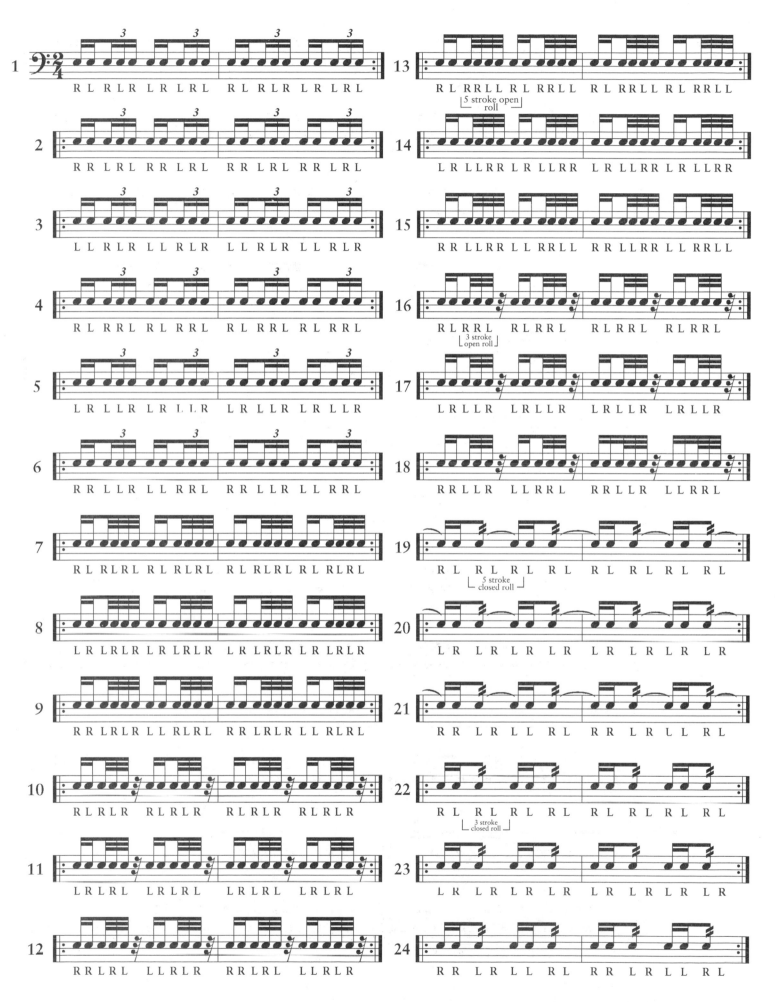

Flam Triplets and Dotted Notes

* Dotted eighths and sixteenths must be given their exact value.
This measure should not be confused with the following:

Flam Triplets and Dotted Notes

Flam Triplets and Dotted Notes

Short Roll Progressions

Short Roll Progressions

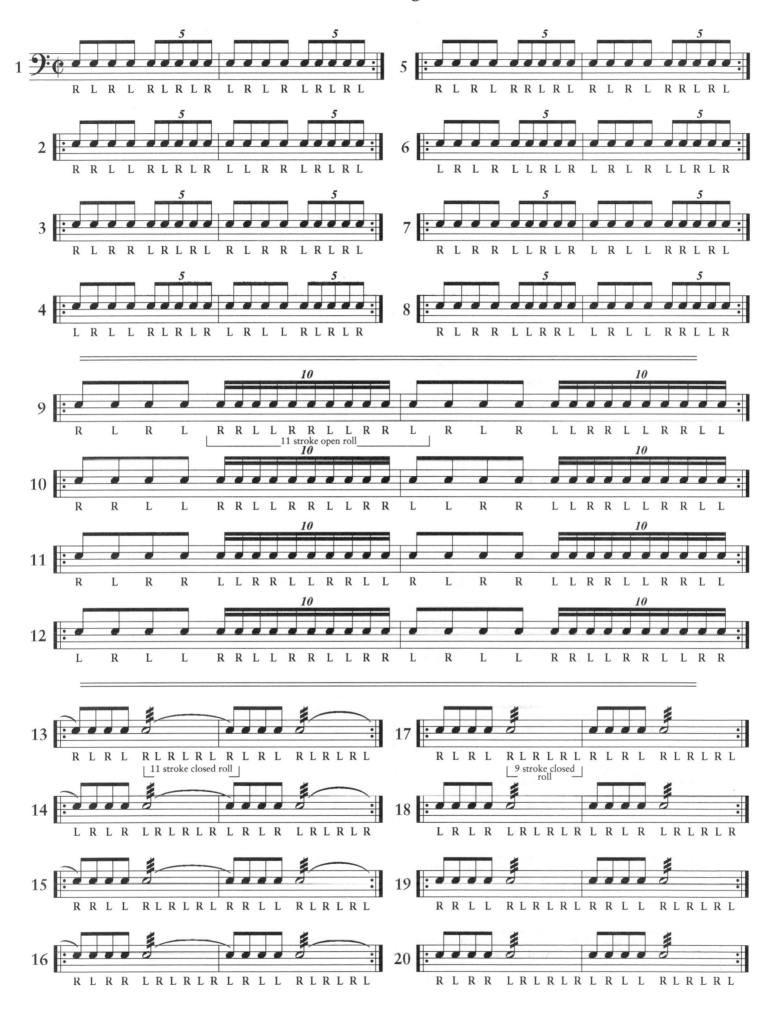

Short Roll Progressions

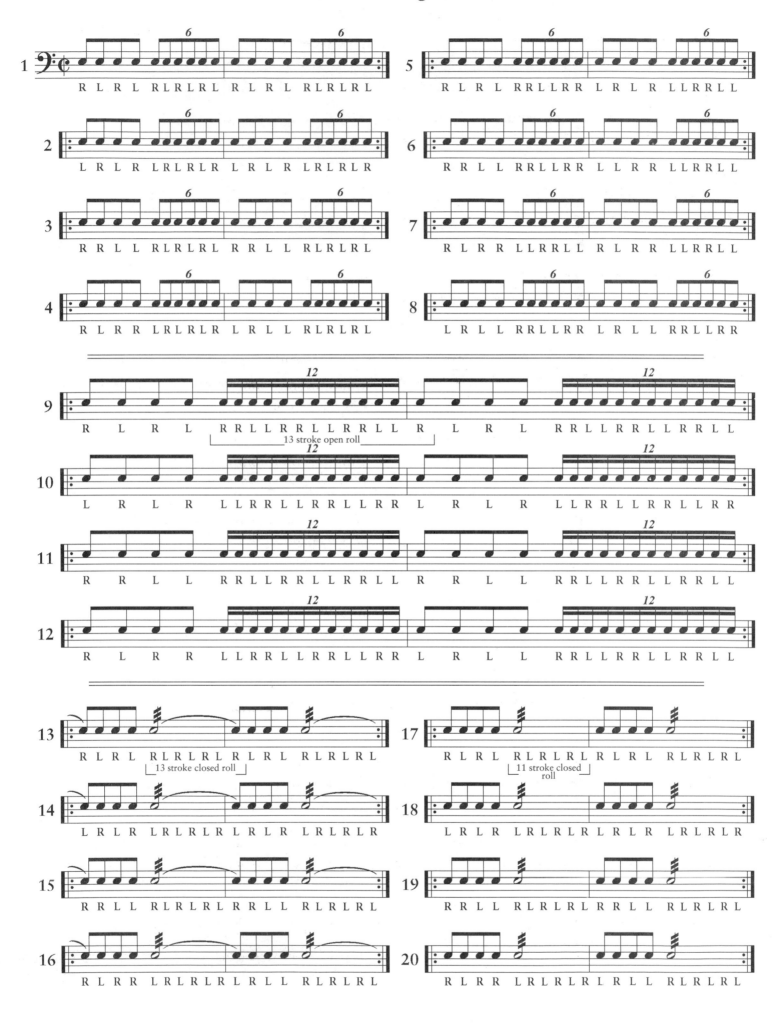

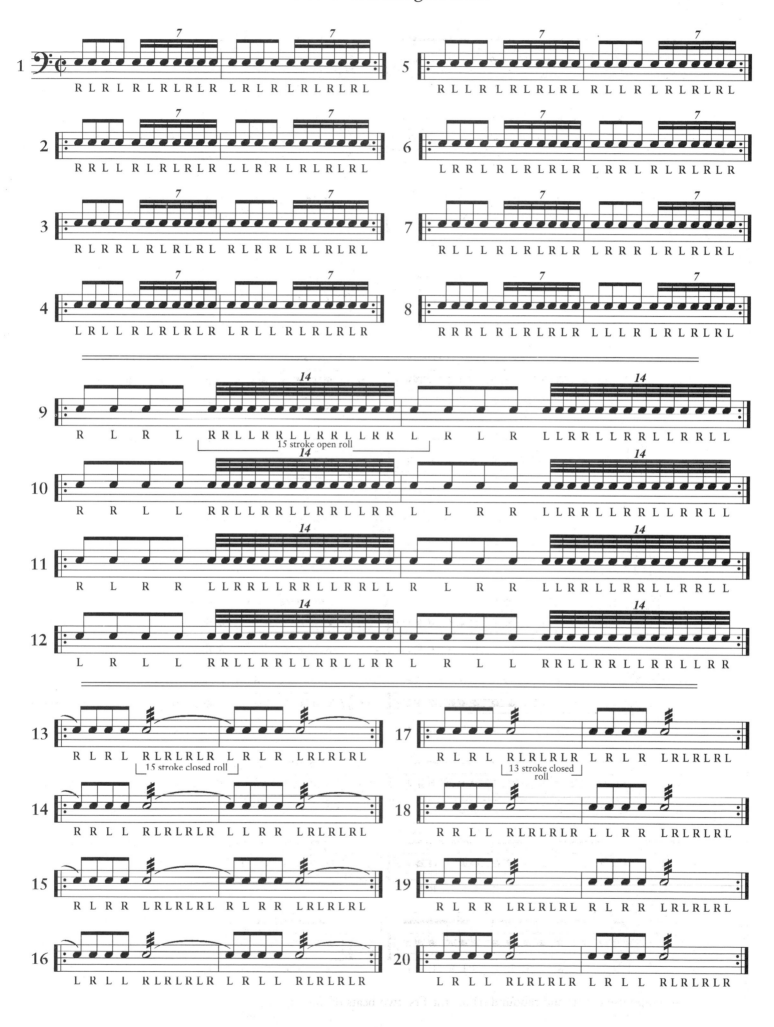

Short Roll Progressions

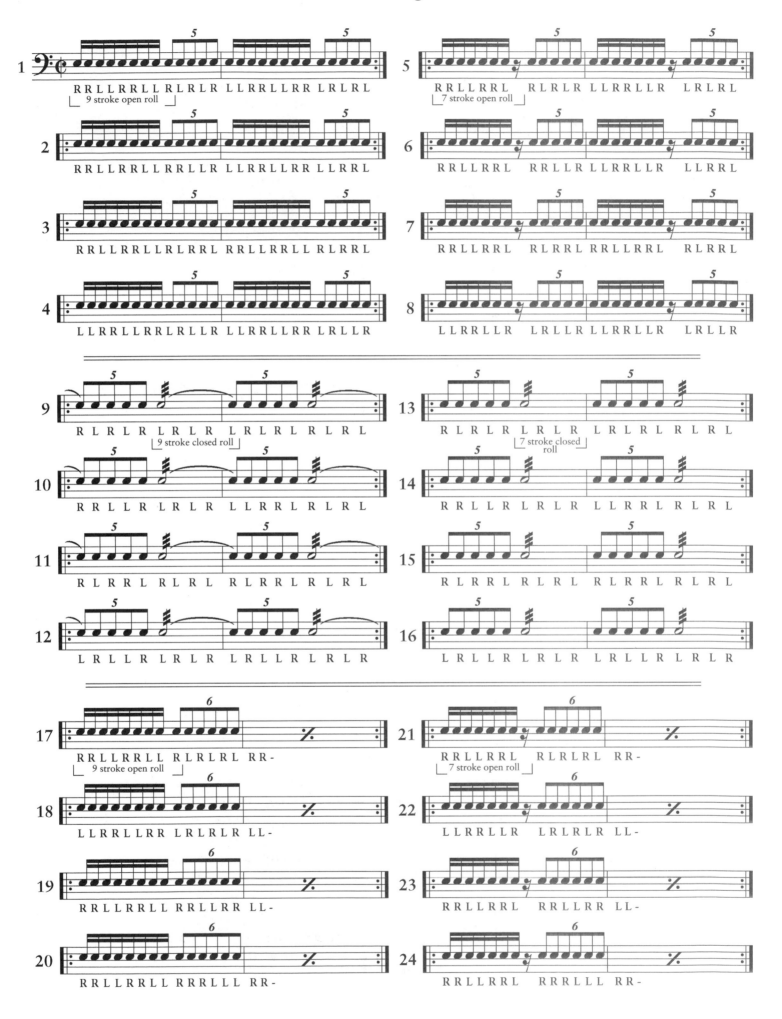

Short Roll Progressions

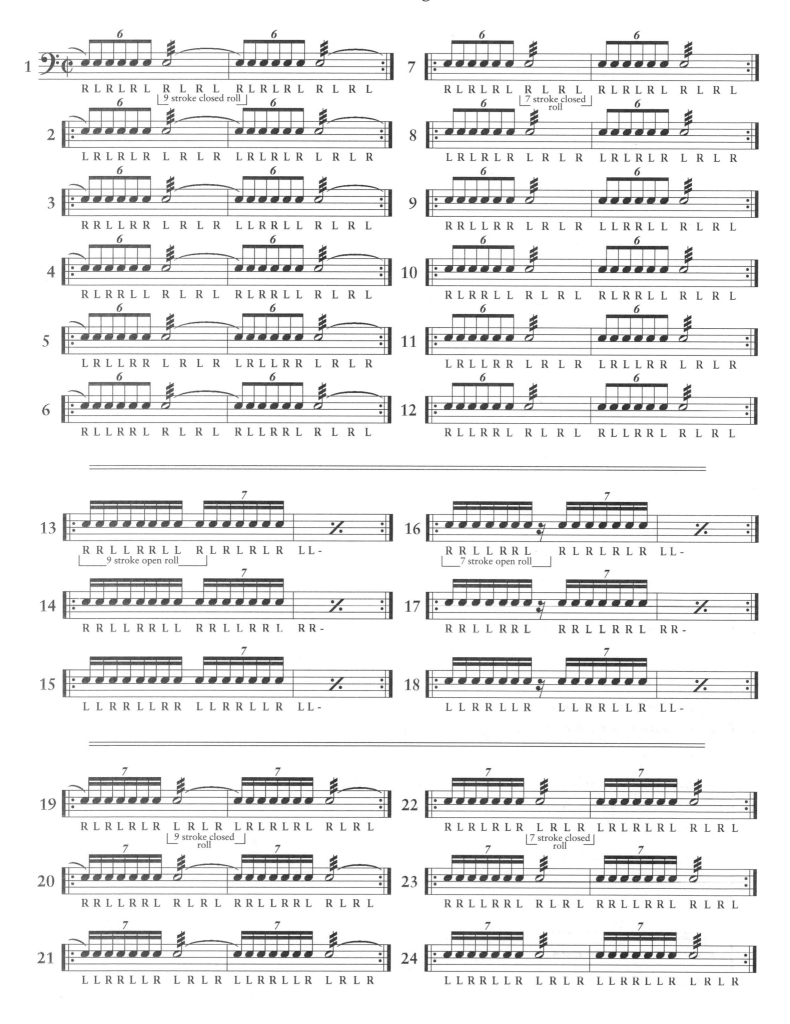

Short Roll Progressions and Triplets

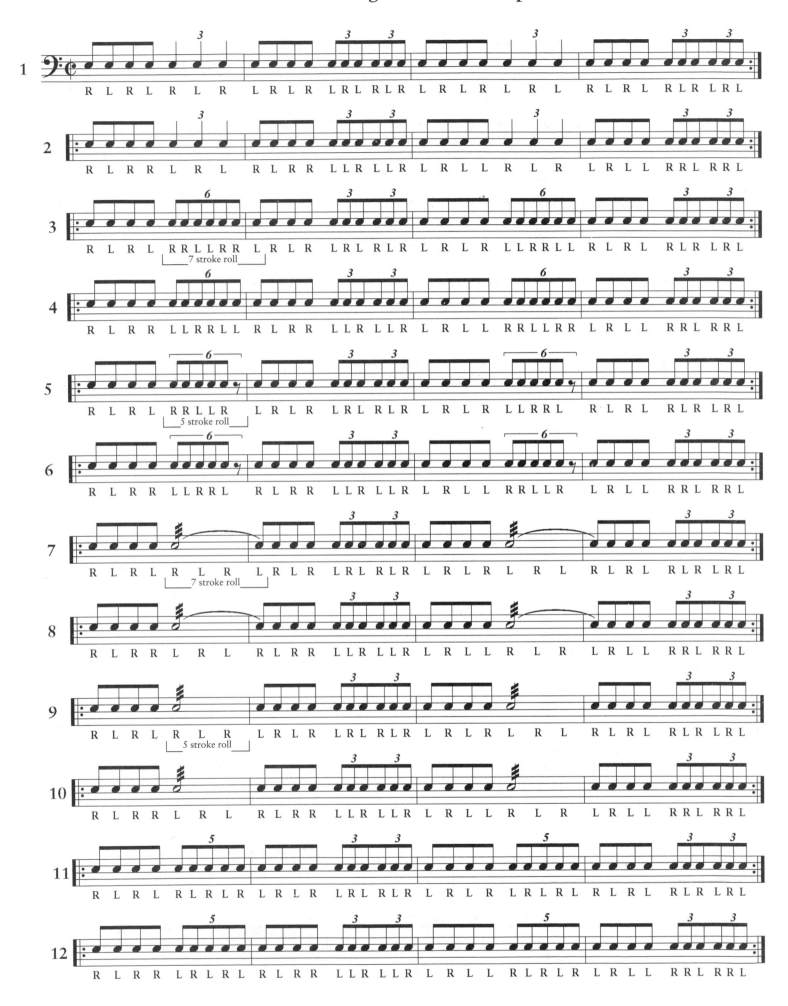

Short Roll Progressions and Triplets

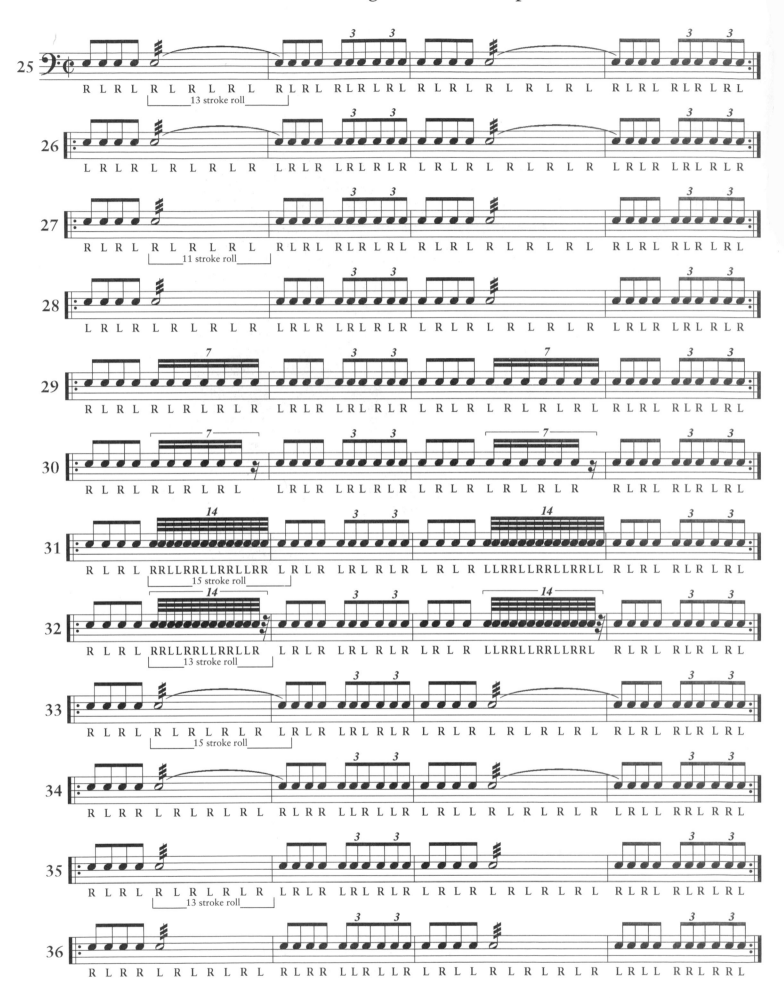

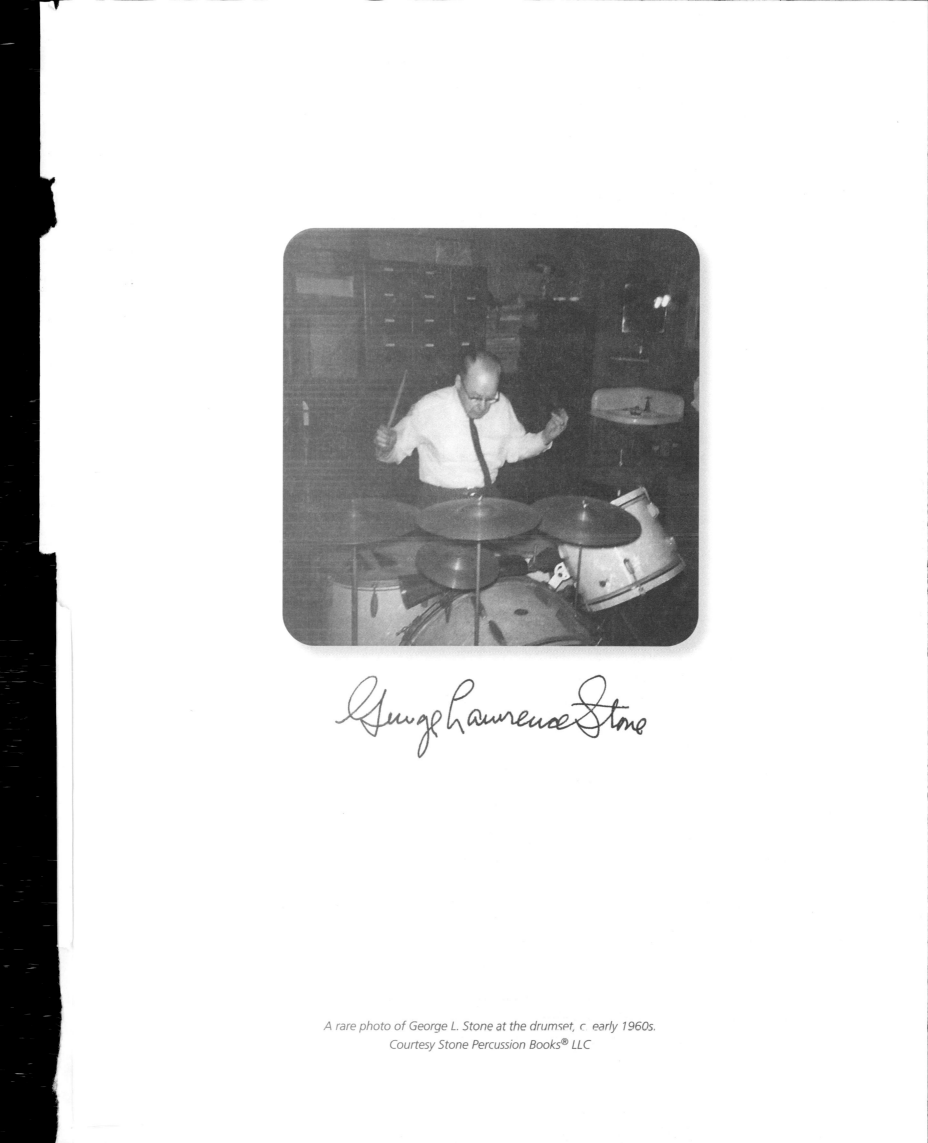

A rare photo of George L. Stone at the drumset, c. early 1960s.
Courtesy Stone Percussion Books® LLC

If you've made it this far, congratulations! Next check out
Accents and Rebounds for the Snare Drummer,
Stone's followup to *Stick Control for the Snare Drummer*

Accents and Rebounds
offers more advanced exercises and includes text from John Riley and Dom Famularo
plus a detailed study guide from Danny Gottlieb and Steve Forster

STONE PERCUSSION BOOKS® LLC
ORIGINALLY PUBLISHED BY GEORGE B. STONE & SON, INC.

www.stonepercussionbooks.com
stonepercussionbooks@comcast.net

Stone Percussion® and Stone Percussion Books®
are trademarks registered with the U.S. Patent and Trademark Office